Great PRAYERS *by* GREAT *people*

30 DAY DEVOTIONAL BY
OSIEN SIBANDA

SIBANDA
PUBLISHING

CONTENTS

Introduction 5

1 God is a Prayer Away 7

2 The First Time Men Prayed 10

3 Isaac's Prayer 13

4 Rebekah's Prayer 16

5 Jacob's Prayer 19

6 Moses Prays to See The Promised Land 21

7 Joseph's Prayer Life 23

8 Jabez's Prayer 26

9 Hannah's Prayer 29

10 Elijah Prays for Rain 32

11 Elijah Requests for Death in Prayer 34

12 Hezekiah's Prayer 37

13 Jonah's Desperate Prayer for Deliverance 40

14 Solomon Prays for Wisdom 43

15 Samson Prays for Strength 45

16 Jehoshaphat's Prayer 47

17 Daniel's Prayer of Defiance 49

18 David's Prayer of Repentance 51

19 Jesus' Prayer for Lazarus 54

20 Jesus' Prayer for The Church 56

21 Jesus' Prayer in Gethsemane 58

22 Mary's Prayer 61

23 The Tax Collector and the Pharisee's Prayer 64

24 The Disciples Prayer 67

25 Stephen's Last Prayer 69

26 Cornelius' Prayer 71

27 Paul Prays for Himself 74

28 Paul Prays for The Philippians 77

29 Paul Prays for The Ephesians 80

30 Husband's Prayer 83

INTRODUCTION

People have very strange ideas about prayer. Many feel that prayer is a certain sound that must terrify the devil or cause God to drop what ever he is doing and attend to them. Some think it should be in Shakespearean English, rich in theological terminology very often spoken very loudly and with a measure of authority. Some believe that the more one shouts in prayer the quicker God will respond to them. Others feel that one should use the Old King James language of 'thy son prayeth, Lord!' Others feel prayer is something that takes place in a certain place or with a certain posture. Others think you must wear something, cover your head, kneel down, carry a rod, or something that signifies seriousness. But none of these things are requirements for true prayer.

The only helpful thing in prayer is what David calls, *"a broken spirit: a broken and contrite heart"* (**Psalm 51:17**). Nothing outside the heart can influence God, not even praying with a Bible on your heart! Prayer has to come from a sincere heart and be in line with God's will. James puts it this way, in The Message Version of the Bible: *"The prayer of a person living right with God is something powerful to be reckoned with"* (**James 5:16**). The New International Version says, *"The prayer of a righteous man is powerful and effective."* Here we learn that righteousness contributes to answered prayer, even if it is a whisper like Hannah did. In fact, you can sound holy and polished in your prayer presentation but if your heart is not right, you are just making noise for God. Paul calls it, *"resounding a gong or a clanging cymbal"* (**1 Corinthians 13:1**). Isaiah also teaches us that God refuses to listen to prayers that come from sinful people.

"When you spread out your hands in prayer, I hide my eyes from you; even when you offer many prayers, I am not listening. Your hands are full of blood!" (**Isaiah1:15**). The heart must just be right. More of this can be seen in **Psalm 51** as David was confessing his sin. Because his heart was right, God listened and forgave him.

Speaking to the disciples who had come to him in **Matthew 5** and **6**, Jesus alluded to **Isaiah 1:15**. *"And when you pray, do not be like the hypocrites..."* (**Matthew 6:5**). Why did Jesus say this? I think it is because God wants us to pray with sincerity. Jesus goes on to instruct his disciples to make sure they forgive their debtors if they request for forgiveness from God (**Matthew 6:12**). There are conditions to prayer and we will do well to heed them if we want our prayers to be answered.

The disciples had asked Jesus to teach them to pray, so Jesus taught them not only to pray but how to pray. Prayer can be learned. We learn to pray by associating with prayerful people. John's disciples learned to pray from John. That is what motivated Jesus' disciples to request to be taught to pray. This book is written to be your prayer companion.

May God bless you as you learn from the prayers of men and women who walked with God. You will be encouraged to learn that even great prophets like Moses, Elijah, and even the Son of God himself, have unanswered prayers in their stories.

1

GOD IS A PRAYER AWAY

❦

"What other nation is so great as to have their gods near them the way the Lord our God is near us whenever we pray to him?"
– Deuteronomy 4:7 –

Moses spoke these words centuries ago, reminding his fellow pilgrims how they were privileged to have a prayer-answering God. God was so near to them that they could access Him. The same God is available to us today and is as near to us as a prayer away. He invites us to call to Him: *"Call to me and I will answer you and tell you great and unsearchable things you do not know"* (**Jeremiah 33:3**). God himself is the one asking us to call Him.

The word 'call' has many meanings, some of which are: to cry out loudly; to shout out loudly in order to attract attention; to scream and yell out; to cry out in a loud voice; to request, and to visit. In essence, the Lord is inviting us to attract His attention by shouting out loudly or by calling to Him. He has great and mighty things to show us and to teach us that we do not even know of. If we do not call to Him we will not be shown the great things that were meant for us. These great things are not limited to material benefits because God has a broad spectrum of things to show us.

Isaiah summons us to *"Seek the Lord while he may be found; call on him while he is near. Let the wicked forsake their ways and the unrighteous their thoughts. Let them turn to the Lord, and he will have mercy on them, and to our God, for he will freely pardon"* (**Isaiah 55:6-7**). In this portion of scripture we are encouraged not only to call but also to seek the Lord. To seek means: to search earnestly; to pursue and go after; to hunt for; to have as an objective, and to be in quest of. All these words show an active effort and intention to find. It also implies that there could be hindrances and obstacles to be overcome during the search, until one finds what one is looking for. In this case we must hunt for the Lord. Our prayer lives should have the determination and focus of a hunter. Our target is to spend time with the Lord, to get His attention so that the influence of heaven may permeate every aspect of our lives here on earth.

The same scripture summons us to turn to God. When one turns, he changes direction. We must shift our position and look to God in prayer. When confronted by anything in the coming days we must turn to God. Our thought life matters to God, therefore we must watch out for the thoughts that creep into our minds and challenge any evil thoughts. As we turn to Him, God will have mercy on us. We must draw near to God if we want Him to draw near to us (**James 4:8**). We should desire personal reconstruction of our character so that we may be Christ like in all we do. Prayer is the place where we die to self and allow Jesus to have His way in us and through us. Prayer is like a workshop for our souls where our Father works in us and puts things in the right places. If we spend time in His hands, He loves us and moulds us into the vessels He wants us to be. Let us go on a journey together as we seek His face. Our God is near us!

REFLECT AND PRAY

Are you happy with your prayer life? If not, why not? What steps are you going to take in order to change or improve? If you are happy, what can you do to enhance your prayer life? Are you hunting for God? What are you seeking first? Pray and ask the Lord to help you to pray! The Lord allowed you to be where you are for a reason. Seek Him and you will find it.

2

THE FIRST TIME MEN PRAYED

❦

"Seth also had a son, and he named him Enosh. At that time people began to call on the name of the Lord."
– Genesis 4:26 –

Genesis 4 is a chapter that introduces the first two cases of murder in the history of humanity. But we also see the first instance of men calling on God or praying, as stated in verse 26.

Cain killed his brother in verse 8 of this chapter, after his brother's offering was accepted and his was declined. God came down and disciplined Cain, and instructed men not to kill him in revenge. *"And the Lord said, "Whoever kills Cain, vengeance shall be taken on him sevenfold."* This was to make men realise that they were not to kill their fellow men. Five generations passed without an experience of murder until a man by the name of Lamech was born to one of the great grandchildren of Cain, the first murderer.

The second murder comes to light through Lamech's confession to his wives (by the way, Lamech was the first man to take two wives): *"Lamech married two women, one named Adah and the other Zillah… Lamech said to his wives, 'Adah and Zillah, listen to me; wives of Lamech, hear my words. I have killed a man for wounding me, a young man for injuring me'"* (**Genesis 4:19-24**).

Lamech then appears to boast and to mock God's judgement on the initial murderer, Cain: *"If Cain is avenged seven times, then Lamech seventy-seven times"* (verse 24). This irreverent confession shows how sin was progressing quickly, from the fall of Adam to the slaying of Abel, to marrying two wives and to slaying yet another man and boasting about it. Lamech's depravity surpassed that of Cain and men realised that they had a problem; they were in serious trouble. So they sought help from the only one who could help them – they called out to God: *"At that time people began to call on the name of the Lord"* (verse 26).

The first prayer was necessitated by increasing sin and depravity. Men wanted God to intervene and save them from this trend of ungodliness that was slowly taking over their lives. People started to pray to the Lord in their search for salvation and help to evade evil. They were tired of ungodliness. Somehow, deep in their spirit, men felt that calling on the name of the Lord would save them. They were right. The prophet Joel spoke about it: *"And everyone who calls on the name of the Lord will be saved"* (**Joel 2:32**). This statement by Joel is quoted by Luke in **Acts 2:21** and by the apostle Paul in **Romans 10:13**. We learn from this that the first prayers ever said were for help against depravity and sin, not for requesting blessing. The initial intention of prayer was for God's salvation, purification and cleansing of the human heart from sin. The first prayer sought to return the human soul to his maker, and the Bible teaches us that when we call on the Lord, He answers!

We must learn to take prayer seriously and pray in faith, for we are promised salvation and help when we pray. Men began to pray! Jesus agreed with this and even taught us not to stop praying: *"Then Jesus told his disciples a parable to show them that they should always pray and not give up"* (**Luke 18:1**). Prayer is here to stay if we want the help of God. Prayer is here to stay if we want to curb evil. Men began to pray!

What do you do when you see ungodliness around you? The early men called on God. Determine to call on God about issues of concern to you. Determine to be a person of prayer.

Reflect and Pray

What do you do when you see ungodliness around you? The early men called on God. Determine to call on God about issues of concern to you. Ask God for the grace not to avenge when wronged. Determine to be a person of prayer.

3

Isaac's Prayer

❧

"Isaac prayed to the Lord on behalf of his wife, because she was childless. The Lord answered his prayer, and his wife Rebekah became pregnant."

– Genesis 25:21 –

Isaac was a wealthy man because *"Abraham left everything he owned to Isaac"* (**Genesis 25:5**). But in spite of all the wealth and possessions he had, he could not start a family to enjoy his wealth with. Rebekah, his wife, was an answer to Eliezer's prayer: *"Lord, God of my master Abraham, make me successful today, and show kindness to my master Abraham. See, I am standing beside this spring, and the daughters of the townspeople are coming out to draw water. May it be that when I say to a young woman, 'Please let down your jar that I may have a drink,' and she says, 'Drink, and I'll water your camels too'—let her be the one you have chosen for your servant Isaac"* (**Genesis 24:12-14**).

One may think Rebekah should have found it easy to conceive after she came to Isaac as a result of prayer, but she did not. She was barren to the point that it caused her wealthy husband to seek help from the Lord in prayer.

There are certain things wealth and money cannot do for us. Rebekah was helpless and needed someone to be sensitive to her need. Isaac, as the husband, rose to the occasion and prayed for her. The Lord heard him and gave him his request, and Rebekah conceived.

As we know from the following verses, this pregnancy was not easy until Rebekah asked, *"Why is this happening to me?"* (verse 22), resulting in her calling on the Lord for help. The fact that God grants us our desires does not mean that we do not face difficulties. We will still face challenges, and in those challenges we should go to God in prayer. Sometimes it will require others to lift us up in prayer. For others to pray for us, we must be vulnerable to them. They must know what we are going through. However, we have to be discreet about who we are vulnerable to.

Isaac's prayer was granted even though that was the beginning of restlessness and strife in the family, as both parents seemed to have a favourite son. This blessing required guidance from the Lord every step of the way, and that is done by calling on the Lord. This family is an example of how we must teach our children and helpers the importance of prayer. That way we empower them for life: even when we leave this world, they will continue to call on God in times of trouble. Abraham prayed; his servant prayed; his son, Isaac, prayed; his daughter-in-law, Rebekah, prayed, and even her son, Jacob, prayed. In all these prayers, God granted them their requests.

If God could grant their requests, He can grant yours too. You just need to study their lifestyles to learn how they related with God. Learn from their strengths and avoid their mistakes. Study their faith to learn how to apply your faith.

REFLECT AND PRAY

Are you sensitive to the needs of others? How much time do you invest in praying for people other than yourself or your immediate family? Husbands and wives, how much time do you spend praying for each other and with each other? Are you empowering your children and loved ones in their prayer lives? Ask God to help you to develop a sensitive heart towards the needs of others. Pray together as families and teach your children to pray.

4

REBEKAH'S PRAYER

❧

*"The babies jostled each other within her, and she said,
"Why is this happening to me?" So she went to inquire
of the Lord. The Lord said to her, 'Two nations are in
your womb, and two peoples from within you will be
separated; one people will be stronger than the other, and
the older will serve the younger.'"*
– Genesis 25:22-24 –

The struggle of Rebekah's children was so intense that it was unsettling her spirit. She could tell something was abnormal, even though she could not put her finger on what it was. Have you been through situations that unsettle your spirit? You find yourself troubled and can sense that something is wrong. Do not ignore such experiences, as destiny could lie in what you choose to do or not to do.

Rebekah had this experience during pregnancy and she chose to call on God: *"So she went to inquire of the Lord"* (verse 22). She chose to pray. When you are uneasy about something, call on God and ask what is happening. Certain problems require the help of God to handle and manage. You may be surprised at the answer you will get. By just praying, Rebekah was privileged to receive the news that today we would obtain after going for a scan. *"Two nations are in your womb..."* she was told (verse 23). She had twins and they were fighting in her womb. There was a struggle for birthright before they were even born. Rebekah was then told one of the most unusual of statements: *"...the older will serve the younger"* (verse 24). This was not a natural order, and Rebekah may never have known how to settle this contention. Certain issues will require you to ask God for wisdom in prayer.

Without God's assurance at the place of prayer, the battle that started in the womb could have ended fatally. Rebekah's wisdom allowed for the will of God to be done. We may not have an answer as to why Esau was destined to serve his younger brother, but God knows why. Joseph had the same experience with his brothers. Unless we inquire from the Lord on such complicated issues, we will fail our children.

"If all is well, why am I feeling like this?" This is a question that can help you ask for wisdom from God in prayer. Always remember to check if there is uneasiness in your spirit. This checking is done on your knees at the place of prayer. It could be that you have a complicated problem that requires God to reveal to you the strategy you need in order to deal with the issue. Rebekah emptied out her frustrations and uneasiness at the place of prayer. She acknowledged that what she was feeling was not normal. It took God's supernatural ability to explain to her what was going on.

Rebekah knew where to look for answers concerning her condition. She understood where the solution to this discomfort would come from. She chose to inquire from the all-knowing God. This shows that she was a woman of faith who trusted in God: that's why she went to Him to inquire. She knew that He would answer her. He promises to answer us when we call (**1 John 5:14**). God answered and told Rebekah the great and mighty work which was happening in her womb. Rebekah did not depend on her husband or parents or a friend to inquire for her. She prayed herself. She did not accept the discomfort and let matters take their own course. She sought a solution from the right source. May we learn from her.

REFLECT AND PRAY

Is there anything unsettling you? Are you facing a situation causing you to ask the same question as Rebekah: "Why is this happening to me?" Are you totally dependent on God for solutions or do you rely on others? Pray and ask the Lord to help you to depend on Him alone. Ask Him to reveal to you the strategy for your situation. Call on Him and He will answer you. Grace be multiplied to you.

5

JACOB'S PRAYER

⁓♦⁓

"Then Jacob prayed, 'O God of my father Abraham,
God of my father Isaac, Lord, you who said to me, "Go
back to your country and your relatives, and I will make
you prosper," I am unworthy of all the kindness and
faithfulness you have shown your servant. I had only my
staff when I crossed this Jordan, but now I have become
two camps. Save me, I pray, from the hand of my brother
Esau, for I am afraid he will come and attack me, and
also the mothers with their children.'"
– Genesis 32:9-11 –

This was a desperate prayer from Jacob. He had been told that Esau was on his way to meet him as he returned to his home country. The last time he saw Esau was when they were fighting for their inheritance, a fight which started in the womb and was interpreted through prayer. He prayed because he was afraid. He was uncertain of what Esau would do. Have you ever been in such a situation before? Did you panic trying to do things in your own strength? Jacob was in *"great fear and distress"* (**Genesis 32:7**).

Although Jacob was now a wealthy man, his wealth could not calm his distress and fear! It is only by calling on the Lord that such a problem could be handled. **Psalm 50:15** teaches us to *"call on me in the day of trouble; I will deliver you, and you will honour me."* God answers us so that we can glorify Him. The more we glorify Him for answered prayer the more He answers us and, prayer is the catalyst for that.

Jacob called on the Lord in his time of trouble: *"Save me, I pray, from the hand of my brother Esau, for I am afraid he will come and attack me, and also the mothers with their children"* (verse 11). You may not have an Esau confronting you, but there could be situations that are giving you some shivers. God has given you a way out through prayer. He says to call on Him in your day of trouble. To you, trouble could be a loss of a job, threat of deportation, eviction, divorce, loss of finances or your home, sickness, and all sorts of things; God has promised to deliver you if you call on Him.

Jacob's prayer was answered. God delivered him in his time of fear. When Esau arrived, God had already dealt with his heart. It would be helpful to read chapter 33 to see how the two men met after a long time. God's intervention and deliverance prevented a catastrophic act of revenge. As Jacob was still stressing over what his brother would do, *"Esau ran to meet Jacob and embraced him; he threw his arms around his neck and kissed him. And they wept"* (**Genesis 33:4**). The Lord will cause your enemies not just to embrace you, but to kiss you and bless you! But you must learn to bring your fears and stresses to him in PRAYER.

REFLECT AND PRAY

Do you have any hidden fears? What or who are you afraid of? Why are you afraid? Trust in the Lord and cast all your cares on Him, for He cares for you. **Psalm 55:22** states that the Lord will sustain you if you cast your cares on Him. Be careful about where you cast your cares; call on God. He has not given you the Spirit of fear but of power, love and self-discipline (**2 Timothy 1:7**).

6

MOSES PRAYS TO SEE THE PROMISED LAND

~~~

"At that time I pleaded with the Lord: 'Sovereign Lord, you have begun to show to your servant your greatness and your strong hand. For what god is there in heaven or on earth who can do the deeds and mighty works you do? Let me go over and see the good land beyond the Jordan – that fine hill country and Lebanon.' But because of you the Lord was angry with me and would not listen to me. 'That is enough,' the Lord said. 'Do not speak to me any more about this matter. Go up to the top of Pisgah and look west and north and south and east. Look at the land with your own eyes, since you are not going to cross this Jordan.'"

– Deuteronomy 3:23-27 –

God has taught us that His ways are not our ways and His thoughts are not ours (**Isaiah 55:8**). In **Numbers 12**, God rebuked Miriam and Aaron for speaking against Moses and even told them how special Moses was in His sight (**Numbers 12:8**). But in **Deuteronomy 3**, Moses prayed that God would allow him to see the Promised Land and God responded differently. He said, *"That is enough. Do not speak to me any more about this matter"* (verse 26). Did you know that God sometimes answered Moses negatively? God did not allow Moses to enter the Promised Land because he failed to follow a simple instruction – he struck a rock that he had been told to speak to.

Moses' prayer was an attempt to change God's mind. God refused and told him to go and prepare Joshua for the Promised

Land instead of him: *"But commission Joshua, and encourage and strengthen him, for he will lead this people across and will cause them to inherit the land that you will see"* (verse 28). Can you imagine praying for something and the Lord gives what you have requested to your brother or your assistant instead of you, and then commands you to help them and strengthen them to receive what you wanted and desired? How would you feel?

There are certain requests that will not be granted because of our mistakes, impatience or disobedience. Moses was very close to God. At one point he asked God to forgive Miriam and Aaron, and God granted him that request. This time, God told him not to pray that prayer again. What would you do if you were in Moses' position? Begin to tell God how you put your life on the line for Him by approaching Pharaoh? Tell Him how unfair He is after you have led His children out of slavery? How is your heart attitude when it becomes clear that God will not grant your request? Do you stop praying, like many of us do? Or do you humbly respond and say, "Your will be done"?

REFLECT AND PRAY

What would be your response if God answered your prayer saying, "That's enough. You will not get what you are praying for, but it will be given to your young brother or your sister."

Pray that you consistently obey God so that you do not miss out on great opportunities due to partial or total disobedience.

7

JOSEPH'S PRAYER LIFE

❦

"We both had dreams,' they answered, 'but there is no one to interpret them.' Then Joseph said to them, 'Do not interpretations belong to God? Tell me your dreams.'"

– Genesis 40:8 –

Here were three prisoners in the dungeon of one of Pharaoh's jails, sharing their experiences of the night before. Two of them had dreams but they could not make sense of them. The dreams appeared significant for both the dreamers, but no one was available to interpret them as far as they were concerned. So they told the third prisoner, who happened to be Joseph. Little did they know that they were dealing with a man whose life was formed through interpreting his own dreams. God can use you to be an answer to your world if you take into account Joseph's wisdom and prayer. Before Joseph heard the dreams, he immediately gave the other prisoners hope by indicating that he knew someone who had an understanding of dreams. *"Do not interpretations belong to God?"* Joseph said.

Joseph's declaration that *"interpretations belong to God"* was a very bold statement and a testimony of his faith. This teaches us that he had confidence in his God and was ready to help point the dreamers in the right direction. It seems Joseph had an effective and productive prayer life, (**James 5:16**). We only see such boldness in the likes of the prophets Elijah, Elisha, and Jesus Himself, to name just a few. Prayer will give you confidence in solving people's issues, glorifying God in the process.

In this case, Joseph announced his faith in the living God to unbelievers in jail. "I have a God who can solve problems" is what Joseph seemed to be saying. He was not fazed by the fact that he was in prison. He still knew how big and able his God was, and was ready to make this known even in jail. Sometimes we unnecessarily allow challenges to silence us when God can turn them towards our good. Joseph not only announced his faith, but also quickly acted upon it. He had previous experience of dreams and their meaning, and was confident that the God who had given dreams and interpretations before would do the same for these prisoners (**Genesis 37:5-11**).

Joseph was confident of his interpretations of dreams because he was confident about his prayers and he was confident about his God. He had faith – and faith always pleases God! Prayer will allow God to open His secrets to us so we can be a blessing to the world.

In the next chapter, Joseph is standing before Pharaoh after being recommended by the butler and, again, he is not shy to speak of his faith – this time to Pharaoh. Pharaoh's words to Joseph were: *"'I had a dream, and no one can interpret it. But I have heard it said of you that when you hear a dream you can interpret it.' 'I cannot do it,' Joseph replied to Pharaoh, 'but God will give Pharaoh the answer he desires'"* (**Genesis 41:15-16**). There seems to be a strong emphasis on God in Joseph's life. Looking at his speech before Pharaoh, it suggests that Joseph already knew the dream and its interpretation. He boldly proclaimed: *"God will give Pharaoh the answer he desires"* (verse 16). Joseph already knew that the dream contained some good news for Pharaoh and he assured him of that. This is how we, as believers, should be in our communities.

God will make known the secrets of men to those who fear and honour Him. When we pray, we acknowledge that God is the ultimate master of life, and will grant us amazing abilities. We will then tell the world about His wonders and His love, so that others can find the same peace with God that we have. This is what Joseph did through his prayer life. Please read the story of Joseph and be encouraged by his courage, patience and faith.

Reflect and Pray

Having read the story of Joseph, what attributes of his would you like developed in you? Is it his sincerity, honesty, holiness, patience, mercy or purity? Ask the Lord in prayer and He can give them to you.

8

JABEZ'S PRAYER

❦

*"Jabez cried out to the God of Israel, 'Oh, that you
would bless me and enlarge my territory! Let your hand
be with me, and keep me from harm so that I will be free
from pain.' And God granted his request."*
– 1 Chronicles 4:10 –

From the time mankind started calling on God, people continued to pray for virtually everything and anything they could not handle or change in their lives. This ranged from deliverance from enemies to barrenness of the womb, famines, coronation of kings, guidance, and virtually anything that troubled them. They also prayed in repentance, in worship and in thanksgiving for answered prayers.

Jabez did the same, and prayed to be blessed indeed. There is nothing wrong with asking to be blessed, provided that our motives and heart attitudes are pure. Jabez had the kind of heart that God was ready to bless. Let us work on our hearts until we attain the character that this man had: *"Jabez was more honourable than his brothers"* (verse 9). After he prayed, God responded by granting him his request. This can easily make us believe that anyone who presents requests to God will have them granted. Not necessarily, as we can see from this account. It is important for us to study and closely dissect the content of Jabez's prayer. What did he ask for?

Amongst the requests that Jabez made was a desire to be kept free from evil. In the NIV, verse 10 says *"keep me from harm"*. Some translations say 'harm', others say 'evil'. Probably the Matthew Henry commentary gets it right when it says that Jabez was praying for protection from both hurt and evil: *"That he would keep him from evil, the evil of sin, the evil of trouble, all the evil designs of his enemies, that they might not hurt, nor make him a Jabez indeed, a man of sorrow."*

This must have pleased God because He desires all of us to avoid evil. When Jesus taught us to pray, He said: *"And lead us not into temptation, but deliver us from the evil one"* (**Matthew 6:9-13**). Jabez prayed the will of God concerning his life and God was pleased with him. Always remember to renounce evil when you pray. Pursue holiness in your daily life and ask God for a clean heart and the right spirit just like David did (**Psalm 51:10**).

Other things he prayed for were full and total blessing, enlargement of territory, for the hand of God to be upon his life, and that he would not be in pain. You can have your territory enlarged as well if you learn from this man. God can grant your desires too. There is another side to this story. Verse 9 introduces Jabez to us as a man who was more honourable than his brothers. There is a good reason why his heart is shown to us. Honour and righteousness could be missing from your life, even if you have been praying for some time. Jabez's background may not have been pleasant but he chose to have a pleasant spirit and God granted his request.

Sometimes we are quick to present our requests to God, yet in them all there is no desire for holiness or to turn away from evil. Renouncing evil must be part and parcel of our prayer lives. If we learn that, God will grant us our requests. And when God has blessed us, we should remember to bless others.

REFLECT AND PRAY

Can God call you honourable? How much effort do you put into turning away from evil? Are you living a blessed life? Pray that the Lord will give you a clean heart. Ask Him to enlarge and increase your 'territory' so that you can be a blessing to all those in your sphere of influence.

9

HANNAH'S PRAYER

❦

"Then Hannah prayed and said: 'My heart rejoices in the Lord; in the Lord my horn is lifted high. My mouth boasts over my enemies, for I delight in your deliverance. There is no one holy like the Lord; there is no one besides you; there is no Rock like our God. Do not keep talking so proudly or let your mouth speak such arrogance, for the Lord is a God who knows, and by him deeds are weighed. 'The bows of the warriors are broken, but those who stumbled are armed with strength."
– 1 Samuel 2:1-4 –

This is considered as Hannah's prayer but in actual fact it is her second prayer. The first prayer is mentioned in **1 Samuel 1:10-16**, where she prayed without uttering a word for she was *"in deep anguish"* (verse 10) due to her barrenness and continued provocations from Peninnah. Her second prayer is recorded after God opened her womb and gave her Samuel. Hannah could not hide her joy and excitement.

In this prayer she is giving thanks to God for coming through for her. Peninnah features in the prayer even though her name does not. *"Do not keep talking so proudly or let your mouth speak such arrogance"* (**1 Samuel 2:3**) is a direct jibe at Peninnah. Remember Peninnah had many years of boasting and arrogance about the fact that she could have children while Hannah could not.

Sometimes it is necessary to pray such prayers, especially if the Lord has come through for you! May the Lord put a song of praise in your heart that will result in your enemies becoming part of the lyrics. Part of Hannah's thanksgiving was a warning to her oppressors not to be arrogant *"because the Lord is a God who knows"* (verse 3) and judges us. Hannah teaches us that we can legitimately reprimand others in our time of thanksgiving, if our motive is to glorify God.

Some of you have been oppressed in your countries and places of work. Be encouraged that the Lord will come through for you as you continue to pray. When He does, it is very appropriate to remind those who had troubled you about the faithfulness of our God and His role as our Judge. No one is holy like the Lord. There is none beside Him. He is a God of knowledge and He knows precisely the right time to answer your prayer. The Lord can make poor and He can make rich. We must know our God and learn how to approach Him with our needs in prayer. Hannah poured out her heart to God in her time of need. She then sang her song of joy out in praise to her God after her prayers were answered.

May we not receive our answers and fail to praise the Lord! Learn to sing praises to God when He comes through for you. Rejoice when the Lord has visited you. As you continue to pour your heart out to the Lord, get ready for a song of praise and thanks because God indeed answers prayers. I encourage you to read Hannah's story and see why she prayed in this way.

REFLECT AND PRAY

Is there anyone provoking you? Do not worry. God sees and He knows. He will vindicate you. Do you have something to sing about? Go on and sing your song to the Lord. He delights in your praises.

10

ELIJAH PRAYS FOR RAIN

❧

"Elijah climbed to the top of Carmel, bent down to the ground and put his face between his knees. 'Go and look toward the sea,' he told his servant. And he went up and looked. 'There is nothing there,' he said. Seven times Elijah said, 'Go back.' The seventh time the servant reported, 'A cloud as small as a man's hand is rising from the sea.' So Elijah said, 'Go and tell Ahab, "Hitch up your chariot and go down before the rain stops you."'
– 1 Kings 18:42-44 –

In this scripture, Elijah prayed that it would rain on the land. There had been no rain for about three and a half years, but Elijah was resilient in his prayer. He got down on his knees, bowing so low that his head was between his knees, and prayed for rain. When he thought he had prayed enough, he sent his servant to go and look for the signs of rain – but there were none. Elijah was not discouraged. He went into prayer again and kept sending his servant to look. He did this seven times until his prayer was answered.

Sometimes we give up too soon because we are not resilient. If Elijah had given up at the first or second attempt, the land would have remained dry. This passage teaches us to be persistent when we pray for critical issues. We cannot afford to be lazy or impatient. Jesus illustrated the importance of such resilience in prayer in a parable in **Luke 11:9-13** (NKJV): *"I say to you, though he will not rise and give to him because he is his* *friend, yet because of his persistence he will rise and give him as many as he needs."*

Elijah was very persistent in his prayer for rain. Jesus shows us that sometimes there is a need to be tenacious in certain situations. As you persist, every slight change in the situation can give you reason to hope and believe for even more change. When Elijah heard about the cloud the size of a hand rising from the sea, he knew something was happening. He did not need to wait for rain to know that he had been answered. The cloud was enough to tell him that his persistence had paid off. He sent a message to Ahab, saying: *"Hitch up your chariot and go down before the rain stops you"* (verse 44).

May the Lord help us to be persistent in prayer.

Reflect and Pray

Are you impatient when it comes to waiting for your prayer to be answered? Is there any discouragement lurking in your heart? Do you often feel like giving up in prayer? Ask the Lord to help you to hold on to His Word whilst you wait for an answer to your prayer. Refuse to be discouraged and trust in the Lord with all your heart. Be persistent in your prayer life.

11

ELIJAH REQUESTS FOR DEATH IN PRAYER

❧❧❧

"Elijah was afraid and ran for his life. When he came to Beersheba in Judah, he left his servant there, while he himself went a day's journey into the wilderness. He came to a broom bush, sat down under it and prayed that he might die. 'I have had enough, Lord,' he said. 'Take my life; I am no better than my ancestors.'"

– 1 Kings 19:3-4 –

This passage teaches us an important lesson: that God is a wise God. He will not answer foolish prayers, like Elijah's request to die: *"I have had enough, Lord. Take my life..."* (Verse 4). The Lord had no plans to take Elijah home to heaven yet, so He refused Elijah's request. He still had work for Elijah to do on earth.

This prayer was prayed out of fear! Elijah was afraid – and God knew it. We do this sometimes! When things are difficult and the situation is threatening, we have a tendency to say, "I have had enough!" At this point some people sadly take their lives, some resign from a difficult job, some divorce, some murder and some fall into drugs and alcoholism, because they feel as though there is nothing better for them. It is not wise to lose hope and take matters into your own hands, because your breakthrough might be just around the corner.

Although Elijah wished he could die, at least he went to God with his predicament. And God did respond to his prayer – but not in the way that Elijah wanted. Instead of death, Elijah was given food! Maybe that was what Elijah really needed to pray for. God obviously knew he was hungry, otherwise why offer him food? And perhaps hunger had made Elijah depressed – it can affect our mood. Perhaps that was the last straw, on top of fear and realising that he had been a coward for running away from Jezebel. *"I am no better than my ancestors,"* he whined. Or perhaps God knew that Elijah wasn't serious, because if he really wanted to die, he could have let Jezebel go ahead and kill him just as she had threatened in verse 2 of this chapter: *"So Jezebel sent a messenger to Elijah to say, 'May the gods deal with me, be it ever so severely, if by this time tomorrow I do not make your life like that of one of them'"* [the murdered prophets]. Elijah fled because his life was threatened, but now he was asking God to kill him instead.

Sometimes we wish for death when we can't see hope in the future. This is the time to go to G*od in prayer and seek understanding, like Rebekah. She asked, "Why is this happening to me?"* (**Genesis 25:22**). It is not the time to pray for death; that is an escape mentality. God sent an angel to give Elijah food, saying, *"Get up and eat"* (verse 5). After Elijah ate and slept again, the Lord gave him another meal that strengthened him for a journey of forty days and forty nights (verse 8), and he did not pray death-wishing prayers again.

The Lord will always listen to our prayers, but only answer 'yes' to those that are in line with His will. In this case, God still had assignments for Elijah, so He answered him in line with His purpose. Should Elijah have complained that he was given what he did not ask for? Should Elijah have gone around moaning that God was unfair? Not at all! But we do it a lot of times when we do not get what we want in prayer, even if that is the will of God for us. Sometimes we pray for death and God refuses. When you pray for that car, God might be seeing death or injury for you if you receive it, so you do not get it. When you ask for more money or a new job, God might be seeing your death or destruction if He answers your prayer, so you will not get it. Elijah was asked, *"What are you doing here?"* You could also be asked, "Why are you praying for this? Why do you want this thing so desperately?" It had better not be a reason that carries death in it.

REFLECT AND PRAY

Have you ever felt like taking your own life? Is there someone or something threatening you? Do not fear; the Lord is with you. God has a plan and a purpose for your life, no matter what things look like now. Your life belongs to Him; therefore you are not authorised to take it.

12

HEZEKIAH'S PRAYER

❦

"In those days Hezekiah became ill and was at the point of death. The prophet Isaiah son of Amoz went to him and said, 'This is what the Lord says: put your house in order, because you are going to die; you will not recover.' Hezekiah turned his face to the wall and prayed to the Lord, 'Remember, Lord, how I have walked before you faithfully and with wholehearted devotion and have done what is good in your eyes.' And Hezekiah wept bitterly."

– 2 Kings 20:1-3 –

Hezekiah was a blessed man, because although he was going to die he was told in advance and given time to prepare. Most people don't have that luxury. At least he could organise his affairs and say his goodbyes before death. But Hezekiah was not having it. Instead, he cried to God for more years. Whatever the reason Hezekiah did not want to die, it was important enough for him to weep bitterly and pray for an extension. Hezekiah had actually lived a righteous and godly life, but still he did not feel he was ready to die.

Here is Hezekiah's prayer: *"Remember, Lord, how I have walked before you faithfully and with wholehearted devotion and have done what is good in your eyes"* (verse 3). How many of us can confidently ask God to inspect our lives in this manner? After that Hezekiah wept bitterly, until the Lord changed His mind and gave Hezekiah fifteen more years of life: *"I have heard your prayer and seen your tears; I will heal you"* (verse 5). Do not hesitate to pour out your tears in prayer, if they are genuine. God will see them. This is what we learn from Hezekiah.

The other lesson we should take from this prayer is the importance of a godly life. Hezekiah used his godly life to bargain for mercy. Our salvation does not rest on how godly we are, but godliness should be a product of our salvation. And it helps a lot in prayer – whereas sin is a barrier to prayer. Walk a life that pleases God all the time. You never know when that could turn out to be a platform for your prayers. The Lord healed Hezekiah from a disease that was threatening his life and he was also given fifteen more years to complete his tasks. What a wonderful way to live, knowing exactly when you will die, so you can confidently make plans for the rest of your time!

As though the promise of healing and longer life was not enough, Hezekiah asked for an unusual sign to confirm that this was definitely going to happen. He needed a concrete form of assurance: *"Hezekiah had asked Isaiah, 'What will be the sign that the Lord will heal me...?"* (verse 8). He did not want to live the next fifteen years of his life sick, so he needed confirmation. Healing was more important for Hezekiah for the next stage of his life. In response, God offered to cause the sun's shadow to go either forwards or backwards ten degrees (verse 10). Hezekiah thought it would be easy for the Lord to turn the shadow forwards, so he asked God to reverse it. The Lord did as asked (verse 11). Why did the Lord do such an amazing thing for this man? Simple. His life must have been very pleasing to the Lord. When we live right, the Lord will encourage us by answering our prayers.

REFLECT AND PRAY

Is your house in order? If the Lord calls you home today, are you ready? Continue to work out your salvation with fear and trembling (**Philippians 2:12**). Currently, is there anything that you are facing that could lead to your demise and eventual death? If you still have a desire to fulfil certain things in your life, you can do what Hezekiah did. Ask the Lord for an extension and trust Him to do what's best for you.

13

JONAH'S DESPERATE PRAYER FOR DELIVERANCE

"From inside the fish Jonah prayed to the Lord his God. He said: 'In my distress I called to the Lord, and he answered me. From deep in the realm of the dead I called for help, and you listened to my cry... When my life was ebbing away, I remembered you, Lord, and my prayer rose to you'... And the Lord commanded the fish, and it vomited Jonah onto dry land."

– Jonah 2:1-10 –

This scene happens deep in the sea, inside the belly of a great fish. Jonah describes the horrors of the scene in verse 5: *"The engulfing waters threatened me, the deep surrounded me; seaweed was wrapped around my head."* This was not a movie scene. Jonah was dying, ready to be digested by a fish. But before the acids broke him down, he called on the name of the Lord his God. He did not find himself in this situation by accident. He had disobeyed by refusing to do what God had sent him to do. Many times the problems we encounter are self-made, as we discount that little inner voice nagging us to avoid certain actions and make different choices.

What is important in this narrative is that Jonah was a believer even though he was disobedient. Jonah's phrase, *"Lord my God"*, indicates to us a man who worshipped God. That is the reason why God sent him in the first place. Many of us believe in God but we are disobedient in the many errands He sends us to do – just like Jonah. This prayer must serve as a warning not to disobey God. He basically scared the hell out of Jonah by putting him in a type of a 'hell' (the fish's belly for three days). Imagine yourself praying in the belly of a giant crocodile, hippo or python, because you have been disobedient. Learn your lessons before it is too late!

Jonah had every reason to thank God because naturally speaking, there was no way he could have escaped the waters of that sea. He was a dead man. The mercy and faithfulness of God is what we must appreciate in this case. He chose to save His servant by allowing Jonah to be swallowed but not to die, and then by commanding the fish to spit him out on dry land. The fish instantly obeyed God, yet the prophet of God disobeyed! It is very sad if animals do the will of the Father but the very people He redeemed fail to.

This prayer must be memorised so that we can learn to obey God on the spot. It is very dangerous to think we can always escape the jaws of a lion, or in this case the digestive system of a fish, every time we mess up. While we applaud God's faithfulness and His great abilities to plan such an escape, we must consider the reason why Jonah was here in the first place. We should focus on this and try to avoid the same mistake. In reading the entire account you will realise that this disobedience cost the ship's crew their cargo, and almost their lives. He almost destroyed innocent people in his disobedience. As you read the story of Jonah, realise that your destiny is linked to other people and your disobedience will affect your fellow brothers and sisters in the faith. Determine not to behave like Jonah.

REFLECT AND PRAY

Have you been diligent to do what God asks you to do in His Word? When He sends you on an errand, do you go? Repent from today and begin to obey God even if you do not agree with what He says. Pray and ask the Lord to teach you to obey His instructions. Do not jeopardise the destiny of others by your disobedience.

14

SOLOMON PRAYS FOR WISDOM

❧

"Now, Lord my God, you have made your servant king in place of my father David. But I am only a little child and do not know how to carry out my duties. Your servant is here among the people you have chosen, a great people, too numerous to count or number. So give your servant a discerning heart to govern your people and to distinguish between right and wrong."
– 1 Kings 3:7-9 –

Solomon began as a humble leader who understood that he needed God's help in order to be an effective leader. His confession was that he did not know how to carry out the duties of kingship, therefore he needed God's help. This led him to pray. Many of us may pray for positions of influence, but sometimes when we are in those positions of leadership we neglect to pray. Don't make that mistake.

Solomon prayed for a discerning heart. A discerning heart is a wise heart. **Proverbs 4:7** teaches us this important attribute for leadership: *"The beginning of wisdom is this: get wisdom. Though it cost all you have, get understanding."* Solomon prayed for the most important thing of all and the Lord was pleased with him. In answer to this prayer, God also added other things to Solomon which he had not asked for, because with wisdom you can handle anything. God said: *"I will give you what you have not asked for – both wealth and honour..."* (**1 Kings 3:13**). When we learn to pray for godly things, God will always add what goes with godliness. Jesus put it this way: *"But seek first his kingdom and his righteousness, and all these things will be given to you as well"* (**Matthew 6:33**). The prayer of Solomon teaches us that God does add certain things to us if our prayers are in line with His will.

It is important to understand the essence of Solomon's prayer about a discerning heart, so that we may also know the things that motivate our God. This phrase, "a discerning heart", suggests not only the willingness and patience to listen to all sides of an issue, but also the desire for the ability to reason. This is evidenced by the way Solomon handled the matter between two women who were fighting over a child (**1 Kings 3:16-28**). We have learned that God answered Solomon's request in abundant measure, granting him not only a discerning heart, but one that was wise for handling the crucial affairs of life in a fair and skillful manner. You can also be a Solomon in your community and place of work, because his abilities came from the same God that you serve.

REFLECT AND PRAY

Are you a wise person? Are you discerning? How do you lead yourself and others? Pray and ask God for wisdom and discretion in all your dealings.

15

SAMSON PRAYS FOR STRENGTH

❦

"Then Samson prayed to the Lord, 'Sovereign Lord, remember me. Please, God, strengthen me just once more, and let me with one blow get revenge on the Philistines for my two eyes.' Then Samson reached towards the two central pillars on which the temple stood. Bracing himself against them, his right hand on the one and his left hand on the other, Samson said, 'Let me die with the Philistines!' Then he pushed with all his might, and down came the temple on the rulers and all the people in it. Thus he killed many more when he died than while he lived."

– Judges 16:28-30 –

Samson was the last of the Judges of Israel, who had been empowered with great abilities and demonstrations of power by the Spirit of God. In Samson's case, he was expected to abide by a particular lifestyle but unfortunately, as happens with many of us, Samson failed and found himself stripped of his power and both his eyes removed.

In this prayer, Samson expresses his pain at losing his sight. He prayed that God would restore his strength so that he could pay back the Philistines for their cruelty: *"Please, God, strengthen me just once more, and let me with one blow get revenge on the Philistines for my two eyes"* (verse 28).

Even though he had messed up before, Samson understood that asking God for the power to overcome evil would be granted. The Philistines were evil people who perpetrated a lot of ungodly deeds against the children of Israel. Samson wanted to make up for having failed God. His calling was to defend the Israelites – and here he was, unable to protect them unless God intervened. He demonstrated that calling upon God and believing that He would help does work. We can overcome our weaknesses and mistakes in prayer.

Samson's attitude and prayer did not just help him destroy more Philistines at his death than he had killed in his life. His prowess and faith is recorded in the list of heroes of faith in **Hebrews 11**: *"And what more shall I say? I do not have time to tell about Gideon, Barak, Samson and Jephthah, about David and Samuel and the prophets, who through faith conquered kingdoms, administered justice, and gained what was promised; who shut the mouths of lions, quenched the fury of the flames, and escaped the edge of the sword; whose weakness was turned to strength; and who became powerful in battle and routed foreign armies"* (verses 32-34). All this happened because these men prayed and trusted God. You can do the same in your generation if only you can learn to call on God in prayer.

Reflect and Pray

Pray to the Lord and ask for the grace not to fall. Call on God and reclaim any lost territory in your life. Ask the Holy Spirit to help you to keep the faith and not to give in to satanic pressures.

16

JEHOSHAPHAT'S PRAYER

"After this, the Moabites and Ammonites with some of the Meunites came to wage war against Jehoshaphat. Some people came and told Jehoshaphat, 'A vast army is coming against you from Edom, from the other side of the Dead Sea. It is already in Hazezon Tamar' (that is, En Gedi). Alarmed, Jehoshaphat resolved to enquire of the Lord, and he proclaimed a fast for all Judah. The people of Judah came together to seek help from the Lord; indeed, they came from every town in Judah to seek him."
– 2 Chronicles 20:1-4 –

The last testimony of Asa, Jehoshaphat's father, states that *"Asa was afflicted with a disease in his feet. Though his disease was severe, even in his illness he did not seek help from the Lord, but only from the doctors"* (**2 Chronicles 16:12**). There is nothing wrong with seeking medical help, but we should seek the Lord first. This failure to seek God for severe challenges led to Asa's death, resulting in his son, Jehoshaphat, taking over the kingship in Israel. Unlike his father Asa, who died because he tried to rely on man to solve his problems, Jehoshaphat knew that any challenge he faced that appeared too big for him was not his to fight: it was the Lord's. For that reason we see him mobilising the entire nation in prayer.

God is always ready to rescue us when men treat us unjustly, but we must call on Him. Jehoshaphat had a good relationship with God and he knew the Word. His prayer was a call to God to remember His promises. After he led the prayers, the Spirit of the Lord came upon one of the men, Jehaziel, in the prayer meeting and he declared the good news from the Lord. The Lord told them not to fear and that this particular battle was not theirs but the Lord's. If they had not prayed, they would have fought a battle that did not belong to them. They would have been defeated.

David also knew the importance of prayer. In **Psalms 27:4**, he says, *"One thing I ask from the Lord, this only do I seek: that I may dwell in the house of the Lord all the days of my life, to gaze on the beauty of the Lord and to seek him in his temple."* To "seek" God or "inquire" (NKJV) is to pray about matters that are not clear, matters that alarm you, and issues that afflict you. God will always help you when you inquire in prayer. Some battles are not ours as children of God because they are too big for us. When they are too big they require our God to take care of them. We must learn to seek God about every challenge, so that we do not panic. The Lord told them not to fear. This came about through prayer and fasting. Learn to follow in Jehoshaphat's footsteps. Praying will always help you to understand that you have a God who is ready to deliver you and to guide you.

REFLECT AND PRAY

Read the story of Jehoshaphat from chapter 16 when he took over from his father, and see the power of prayer. Are there any armies and tough situations confronting you? They may just be for the Lord not you; but you will not know until you take time to pray. Jehoshaphat was alarmed before he prayed, but when the Lord answered him, he appointed men to sing some of the most powerful words of worship: *"Give thanks to the Lord, for his love endures for ever"* (**2 Chronicles 20:21**). Many people have written worship songs using Jehoshaphat's words.

17

DANIEL'S PRAYER OF DEFIANCE

❧❧❧

"Now when Daniel learned that the decree had been published, he went home to his upstairs room where the windows opened toward Jerusalem. Three times a day he got down on his knees and prayed, giving thanks to his God, just as he had done before."
– Daniel 6:10 –

The story of Daniel is an amazing story of a believer who would not compromise his faith for anything. His life was characterised by prayer and devotion to God. In a foreign land, Daniel found solace and guidance from God through prayer. Never underestimate the power of prayer.

Daniel not only adhered to his faith and his God, he was also circumspect in obeying the laws of the land. Because of that, his enemies knew how to offend and attack him. They were aware that when the law of the land conflicted with the law of his God, Daniel would choose the law of God. This is the context of **Daniel 6:10**. Daniel continued to pray to the Lord, even though to do so was now against the law of the land in which he lived.

Undeterred by the royal proclamation that banned praying to any god apart from the god of Nebuchadnezzar, Daniel continued to open his windows so anyone could hear that he was still praying to the Lord, just as he always did. And not just once – he prayed three times a day, as was his custom. The lesson from this is that prayer was such a vital part of Daniel's life that he was prepared to die for it. The account states that he was thrown into the den of lions to punish him for praying to the living God. God closed the mouths of the lions and his enemies were silenced.

Daniel's story teaches us that God will always be committed to us if we are committed to him. In this case, the commitment was consistently praying to God. We are not told what Daniel was praying for three times a day, but we are aware that his actions landed him in a den of lions. Daniel was not fazed at all. Many of us have not been in such a dire situation, yet we fail to pray. Throughout this series, we have been highlighting the importance of prayer and the fact that God answers prayer. Prayer also indicates to the world our belief in God and His ability to meet our needs through His mighty power.

Sometimes we are tempted to disregard our faith, but Daniel knew that his life could only be meaningfully sustained through a sound relationship with God. As the narrative unfolds, Daniel ends up helping the king with the interpretation of his dreams. The very man the officials were trying to kill was the one who ended up helping their king. Don't be discouraged in your prayer life. One day those hours you invest in prayer will bring the salvation of your family and community.

The story does not end there. Daniel was eventually appointed as the second-in-charge to the king of Babylon. The only reason this happened was because of his prayers. God rewarded him by making him influential, and eventually ushering salvation to Babylon. Don't stop praying. The Lord will surely visit you and make you a blessing.

REFLECT AND PRAY

Please read the story of Daniel and learn the significance of an unwavering faith. Ask God to give you the resilience and courage of Daniel.

18

DAVID'S PRAYER OF REPENTANCE

৻৵৶৽৾

"Have mercy on me, O God, according to your unfailing love; according to your great compassion blot out my transgressions. Wash away all my iniquity and cleanse me from my sin. For I know my transgressions, and my sin is always before me."

– Psalm 51:1-3 –

The prayer in this psalm is associated with one of the hardest experiences in David's life, after his affair with Bathsheba and the subsequent murder of her husband, Uriah, in an effort to cover it up. This sin was exposed by the prophet Nathan who courageously confronted David about it.

Repentant prayer begins with an admission of guilt, followed by a plea for God's mercy. The essence of this prayer is a request for mercy. David needed God's mercy and forgiveness. We must learn to confront our sins and iniquities in our prayer time before the Lord. Mercy and forgiveness are God's gift to a confessing sinner. Confessed sins are cleansed by the blood of Jesus through the sacrifice of the cross, allowing God to work with us again. In verse 6 of the same Psalm, David states that God requires *"truth in the inward parts"* (NKJV). He also asks to be cleansed with hyssop, and to be thoroughly washed clean. We must be truthful about our sin and not gloss over it. We must ask the Lord to purge us thoroughly from that sin. Repentance means we are turning away from sin and forsaking that sin, instead of saying we are sorry then continuing to commit the same sin.

At one point Jesus showed the link between forgiveness and healing. *"'Which is easier: to say, "Your sins are forgiven," or to say, "Get up and walk"? But I want you to know that the Son of Man has authority on earth to forgive sins.' So he said to the paralysed man, 'I tell you, get up, take your mat and go home'"* (**Luke 5:23-24**). This shows us that healing is sometimes linked to the forgiveness of our sins. This can only occur if we are sincere enough to bring them before God in prayer. Some difficult situations are not dealt with because of the presence of sin in our hearts.

David's penitent prayer teaches us to take repentance seriously if we want the Holy Spirit to flow in and through us. Sometimes we have a tendency to skim through our confessions because we are ashamed. We want to get them out of the way quickly, so that we can make progress and ask for what we want. But we can never make progress until we are sure that our sin has been dealt with. David was sincere and broken in his repentance, and that is what God requires, according to **Psalm 51:17**: *"My sacrifice, O God, is a broken spirit; a broken and contrite heart you, God, will not despise."* So the prayer of repentance must be taken seriously and done sincerely.

David teaches us to take time to deal with our sin in prayer, and then God will forgive us and restore our relationship with Him. Remember that the first sermon Jesus preached began with the word, *"Repent..."* (**Matthew 4:17**), the first thing the apostles told the people to do was repent (**Acts 2:38**), and repentance was the central theme of John the Baptist's ministry. So we must be serious about turning away from sin.

REFLECT AND PRAY

How often do you confront your heart? Do you often repeat the same sins? Are there any areas in your life where you are not walking in truth? Ask the Lord to help you to repent genuinely. Renew your mind with the Word of God and apply it in order to avoid repeating sin. Take the consequences of sin seriously, because at the end of it all the wages of sin is death!

19
JESUS' PRAYER FOR LAZARUS

❦

"So they took away the stone. Then Jesus looked up and said, 'Father, I thank you that you have heard me. I knew that you always hear me, but I said this for the benefit of the people standing here, that they may believe that you sent me.' When he had said this, Jesus called in a loud voice, 'Lazarus, come out!' The dead man came out..."
– John 11:41-44 –

This is one of the few instances where Jesus prayed to the Father in full view of a crowd. He did this so that the people would believe that He came from God: *"I said this for the benefit of the people standing here, that they may believe that you sent me"* (verse 42). Sometimes God answers our prayers to help other people believe that we are His disciples. Jesus started His prayer by thanking God for having heard Him. This shows us that Jesus had already prayed for Lazarus well before He met the crowd by his grave, otherwise when would the Lord have heard him? He began: *"Father, I thank you that you have heard me. I knew that you always hear me..."* (verses 41-42).

Jesus demonstrated a very important point in prayer – that of a sustained, confident and knowledgeable relationship with the Father. He was so confident about His relationship with the Father that He told the crowd in His prayer about it. He was also so confident that the Father always hears Him that he raised His voice for them to hear Him call Lazarus out of the grave. This is a very important lesson, especially considering the results of His prayer in Gethsemane: *"Father, if you are willing, take this cup from me..."* (**Luke 22:42**). God heard Jesus in this prayer, but He did not take the cup away because it was not God's will to take it away. It might have been Jesus' human desire and He made that desire known to God, but God's will had to be supreme.

God always hears our prayers. The fact that God hears is motivation and encouragement enough for us to pray. But hearing our prayers is not the same as answering our prayers. Sometimes God will not give us the answer we are looking for, but that does not mean He did not hear us or that He does not care. Jesus teaches us here that God does indeed hear every prayer and then answers according to His will. In the case of Lazarus, God granted Jesus' desire by raising Lazarus from the dead. This helped those standing by to understand and believe that Jesus was the Son of God. Remember that Jesus had already promised the family that Lazarus would rise again (verse 23). As His disciples, we must learn to develop a confident relationship with Him, both privately and publicly. Our problem is that we do not have an intimate relationship with Jesus yet we expect Him to suddenly come through with big miracles in public. It is those people who know their God who will *"carry out great exploits"*, according to **Daniel 11:32** (NKJV).

REFLECT AND PRAY

Do you believe that God always hears you? Are you confident that the Father will grant you what is best, not necessarily what you want? Do you trust in God no matter the outcome of your prayer requests? God has great plans for you and they will come to pass. Trust in His goodness and love for you and do not lean on your own understanding.

20

JESUS' PRAYER FOR THE CHURCH

❧

"My prayer is not for them alone. I pray also for those who will believe in me through their message, that all of them may be one, Father, just as you are in me and I am in you. May they also be in us..."

– John 17:20-21 –

John 17 is one of the final chapters where Jesus prayed. First He prayed for Himself, then He prayed for His disciples, and then finally, from verse 20, for all believers. That includes us, as He prayed for all those who would believe in the future, through the disciples' message.

Jesus first prayed for our unity: *"I pray... that all of them may be one"* (verses 20-21). This unity takes place through the sanctification of believers. This is what Jesus desired here! His followers are to love one another in order for the world to believe in Jesus (verse 21). This loving relationship of believers towards one another is the greatest witness for Jesus Christ. **John 13:35** confirms this: *"By this everyone will know that you are my disciples, if you love one another."*

Jesus wants us to be just as unified as He is with His Father... *"just as you [His Father] are in me [Jesus] and I am in you"* (verse 21). This is impossible in our own strength. We need Jesus in us, by His Spirit, so that we can truly love one another and remain in the love of God. This is why Jesus sealed this important part of our faith walk in this prayer. We must also continue to pray in this manner and make sure we are in

Christ always. The Trinity's unity is our example as the body of believers. If any one of these is missing then there ceases to be unity. Remember that the Father, the Son and the Spirit are already united. What they are doing in essence is to unite us to their unity, but they also call on us to unite with our brothers and sisters in the Lord.

So it is essential for us to know the love of God if we are to replicate it among the Church, thus drawing all men to Jesus. In **Galatians 3:28**, Paul says, *"There is neither Jew nor Gentile, neither slave nor free, nor is there male and female, for you are all one in Christ Jesus."* We should not see each other according to the flesh, but according to the spirit. We are now all one in Christ Jesus and that's what should unite us. United we stand but divided we will fall. There are more benefits when we are united than when we allow disunity and discord. **Psalm 133** tells us that God commands a blessing where there is unity. We must make every effort to be one, as this is what pleases the Lord. It was Jesus' dying wish that we all love one another and be one. When we are not united we are actually walking in disobedience, and that does not please the Lord.

In verse 24, Jesus also prayed for us to be with Him in the future. This prayer gives us the sure hope of meeting Him in glory if we continue to obey what He says.

Reflect and Pray

Are you walking in unity with your fellow believers? Is there unity in your home? Do you obey the commandment of love? How are your relationships with your family, both natural and spiritual? Ask the Lord to help you to walk in unity. Pray that you may be loving and caring. Pray that you may not cause discord.

21

JESUS' PRAYER IN GETHSEMANE

❧

"Jesus went out as usual to the Mount of Olives, and his disciples followed him. On reaching the place, he said to them, 'Pray that you will not fall into temptation.' He withdrew about a stone's throw beyond them, knelt down and prayed, 'Father, if you are willing, take this cup from me; yet not my will, but yours be done.' An angel from heaven appeared to him and strengthened him. And being in anguish, he prayed more earnestly, and his sweat was like drops of blood falling to the ground."

– Luke 22:39-44 –

Before this experience, Jesus is recorded as going away to pray, indicating to us that prayer was an intricate part of Jesus' life. In **Luke 18** He told a parable that emphasised the importance of prayer for believers. In the account today, Jesus went to the Mount of Olives "as usual" (verse 39). His custom was not to climb the mountain but to pray at the mountain.

As soon as they got to the summit, He instructed His disciples to pray. This was Jesus' custom. In this case, He told them to pray so that they would avoid evil: *"Pray that you will not fall into temptation"* (verse 40). We learn here that one good and effective way of avoiding temptation is prayer.

As far as Jesus was concerned, He had to pray to avoid temptation. Jesus' temptation was to avoid the salvation programme, as indicated in His prayer: *"Father, if you are willing, take this cup from me; yet not my will, but yours be done"* (verse 42). He teaches us to submit our will to God in times of difficulty.

The difficulty He had to face was the ultimate one – a terrible death. In this prayer we see Him agonising over the idea of facing the wrath of God. He had not been on this journey before. He did not want separation from God as He carried the sins of the world. He agonised even after an angel had strengthened Him. The wrath of God was too fearful for Him. Many of us take the wrath of God lightly, yet the Son of God agonised over it in prayer. The cup Jesus was talking about was a figure of speech for the wrath of God due to the sins of mankind. (See **Ezekiel 23:31-34; Jeremiah 25:15-16; Psalm 11:6; Psalm 75:7-8**.)

In this particular prayer, God's answer to Jesus was a refusal of His request to avoid the suffering of the cross. However, God did provide angelic help for Jesus to face what was coming. Sometimes God answers our prayers by eliminating the trials, but at times He answers by providing strength in the middle of the trial or difficulty. Sometimes God does not give light for us in that dark valley, as David pointed out. Instead, He walks through it with us: *"Even though I walk through the darkest valley, I will fear no evil, for you are with me..."* (**Psalm 23:4**). The dispatching of an angel was to show Jesus that God was with Him. Sometimes God will send people to help us walk through these dark and terrible places, because our future will require certain experiences. Jesus needed to die before He could be raised! This prayer teaches us to trust God and ask for His will in times of difficulty. The temptation we must overcome is to run away from God's will when we experience pain and discomfort.

REFLECT AND PRAY

Are you facing any 'cup moment' that you wish would be removed from you? Is there anything or anyone tempting you? Pray that you may not succumb to temptation. Do not compromise. What you compromise to get you will end up losing. If your 'cup' is not removed, rest assured that the Lord will be with you and He will walk with you. He will not abandon you.

22

MARY'S PRAYER

❧

"My soul glorifies the Lord and my spirit rejoices in God my Saviour, for he has been mindful of the humble state of his servant. From now on all generations will call me blessed, for the Mighty One has done great things for me, holy is his name. His mercy extends to those who fear him..."
– Luke 1:46-50 –

In this prayer in the first chapter of Luke (verses 46-55), famously known as the Magnificat, Mary teaches us how to worship God for His faithfulness.

Before this prayer, Mary had an encounter with an angel who had promised her that she would conceive and bear a saviour (verse 36). In verse 37, Mary was told that *"no word from God will ever fail."* By the time of this prayer, Mary had seen the fulfilment of that prophecy, because she was now pregnant without having had any sexual contact with a man! This was not just a miracle for her, it was a wonder! God will make you wonder too.

God keeps His promises no matter how difficult or seemingly impossible things may appear, and this is what Mary teaches us in this prayer. The angel Gabriel's statement about God should be our statement of faith each time we call on God: *"For with God nothing will be impossible!"* (verse 37, NKJV). Mary had just witnessed this. She taught us the importance of humility before God while exemplifying to us a readiness for faithful and obedient service. This should be our character and lifestyle as believers. Learn to obey and believe God. How ready are you to allow God to do what He wants with your life? Can you allow Him even if it threatens your big day? We are not told that Mary had a big wedding after God brought a new life to her womb. Are you ready to trade your dreams for God's purposes? This is what we must learn through Mary.

When Mary came to visit her cousin, Elizabeth, there was a reaction in Elizabeth's womb and this was the beginning of her greatness. John the Baptist (the Messiah's forerunner) gave testimony to the Messiah even before he was born. Both the mothers witnessed this in their encounter, prompting this popular portion of scripture we have just read.

This was a prayer of worship and adoration to God. It was not a prayer to call on God in time of trouble. It was not a prayer asking for deliverance. It was a prayer in response to God's power and faithfulness. These women were privileged to taste the power of heaven and they knew that they had been *"highly favoured"*, as the angel put it in his salutation to Mary (verse 28). How do you pray when you see such a manifestation of God's power? Your soul will glorify the Lord and your spirit will rejoice in the Lord your saviour.

King David had experienced God's wonderful works when he prayed **Psalm 34**: *"Glorify the Lord with me: let us exalt his name together"* (verse 3). He did not want to glorify the Lord alone. He summoned help to bring the Lord the praises due to Him because of His goodness. David felt that his praises alone were not enough.

As you continue to pray and seek the Lord, He will surely visit you with miracles and wonders. Be ready to give Him the glory, as Mary did. You may notice another similar prayer by Hannah in **1 Samuel 2** after she experienced a similar miracle, having lived for a long time without conceiving. Please read these prayers, build up your faith and prepare to glorify God when your time comes, for He shall surely visit you. For with God nothing shall be impossible!

REFLECT AND PRAY

Are there things that God has done in your life whereby you can see His hand? Take time to thank and worship Him. Allow your soul and your spirit to worship Him. Invite people to glorify the Lord with you. See what the Lord will do.

23

THE TAX COLLECTOR AND THE PHARISEE'S PRAYER

❦

"Two men went up to the temple to pray, one a Pharisee and the other a tax collector. The Pharisee stood by himself and prayed: 'God, I thank you that I am not like other people – robbers, evildoers, adulterers – or even like this tax collector. I fast twice a week and give a tenth of all I get.' But the tax collector stood at a distance. He would not even look up to heaven, but beat his breast and said, 'God, have mercy on me, a sinner.'"

– Luke 18:9-14 –

In this example of two praying men, Jesus is warning us about our attitude when we approach God in prayer. We must be humble and seek His mercy, rather than parade our good works. First, the Pharisee never really prayed. He just told God that he was better than others, and why. He didn't request anything from God; he just put other people down and bragged about his good works. That is not prayer! This was just a proud man boasting about what he thought mattered to God. Let us learn how to pray effectively. James teaches us that the *"prayer of a righteous person is powerful and effective"* (**James 5:16**), not the prayer of a proud man. God already knows what we do and what we need (**Matthew 6:8**). We do not have to impress Him with our words.

Praying is communing with God, and includes seeking help for issues that are troubling us. Prayer is not a time to show how superior we are. The content of the Pharisee's prayer reveals his problems: pride, arrogance and self-righteousness. The Pharisee's prayer sounds as if God should be grateful to him for his commitment in obeying God's commandments! Our commitment to God's ways is for our good and the good of others, not for God. This man looked down on other people in front of the very God who created them, and thought God would be impressed by that. That is very dangerous! We must be careful how we look at other people. It can have a bearing on our prayers.

Jesus later warned that we should not exalt ourselves at the altar of prayer (verse 14). The only person worthy of all exaltation is God. *"Hallowed be your name"*, Jesus taught us to pray. The Pharisee was hallowing His name while despising others. Prayer is a place where we recognise and realise that we are sinners needing grace before God, no matter how good we think we are.

The tax collector approached prayer differently: *"God, have mercy on me, a sinner"* (verse 13). This caused Jesus to say that this man left the altar of prayer more justified than the Pharisee. This is an example of an attitude of humility that we must have when we pray. The tax collector knew that he could not say or bring anything to enhance his standing with God. He realised that only God's mercy would make room for him, not his own works. Jesus clearly identified the contrast between these two men as humility and pride, between those who exalt themselves and those who humble themselves.

God will bring down the proud and He will not answer their prayers. He will, on the other hand, lift up the humble and answer their prayers. We can see this in Mary's prayer: *"He has scattered those who are proud in their inmost thoughts. He has brought down rulers from their thrones but has lifted up the humble"* (**Luke 1:51-52**). We must learn this invaluable lesson whenever we approach God in prayer. Please read the whole of Mary's prayer in **Luke 1:46-55**.

REFLECT AND PRAY

How is your attitude when you pray? Are you self-righteous? Do you understand that you can only access God's presence by His grace and mercy, and not your human effort? Pray that you may not walk in pride. Repent of any self-righteousness.

24

THE DISCIPLES' PRAYER

"When they heard this, they raised their voices together in prayer to God. 'Sovereign Lord,' they said, 'you made the heavens and the earth and the sea, and everything in them... Now, Lord, consider their threats and enable your servants to speak your word with great boldness. Stretch out your hand to heal and perform signs and wonders through the name of your holy servant Jesus.' After they prayed, the place where they were meeting was shaken. And they were all filled with the Holy Spirit and spoke the word of God boldly."

– Acts 4:24-31 –

The early church was growing fast and the chief priests, Sadducees and elders were not happy, so they started persecuting the church, in an attempt to stop them preaching the name of Jesus. In this case, a lame beggar had just been healed and there was excitement everywhere. Peter had been arrested and threatened with death if he continued to preach. The disciples got together to bring the matter before God. They had seen many of their brothers beaten and some even beheaded. They needed God to give them boldness and more miracles: *"Now, Lord, consider their threats and enable your servants to speak your word with great boldness. Stretch out your hand to heal and perform signs and wonders..."* (verses 29-30).

At times this is what we need to ask for in prayer: boldness to declare the word of the Lord. When we do so, the Holy Spirit will help us. The early church asked for boldness and the Lord granted it to them immediately: *"After they prayed, the place where they were meeting was shaken. And they were all filled with the Holy Spirit and spoke the word of God boldly"* (verse 31).

This should be our prayer today because we are in exactly the same position and we need boldness to preach. Some of us have stopped to ask for signs and wonders in prayer. The church should always be praying for and anticipating signs and wonders. We must be filled with the Spirit regularly and have our places of worship shaken by the arrival of the Holy Spirit. This should lead to the salvation of souls.

Learn to bring every challenge to God in prayer. He will not only hear, He will answer and strengthen you. The Lord will fill you with His Holy Spirit when you ask Him in prayer.

REFLECT AND PRAY

What is threatening your faith walk today? Bring it to the Lord and ask Him to help you. Ask the Lord to confirm His Word with signs and wonders when you preach the gospel.

25

STEPHEN'S LAST PRAYER

❦

"While they were stoning him, Stephen prayed, 'Lord Jesus, receive my spirit.' Then he fell on his knees and cried out, 'Lord, do not hold this sin against them.' When he had said this, he fell asleep."

– Acts 7:59-60 –

Stephen was full of the Holy Ghost, as evidenced by his desire not to seek revenge. All he wanted was to do the will of the Father and to please Him. He was so consumed with doing the will of the Father that this terrifying moment could not stop him. He fully trusted in the Holy Spirit for the grace to overcome. This came as a result of prayer.

The only other person to forgive His killers in such a way was our saviour, Jesus Christ. Here is His account: *"When they came to the place called the Skull, they crucified him there, along with the criminals—one on his right, the other on his left. Jesus said, 'Father, forgive them, for they do not know what they are doing"* (**Luke 23:33-34**). This heart is what Stephen was emulating, and he imitated Jesus even to the point of his own death. Every believer should have this attitude. It is called a Spirit-filled life, which results from prayer and walking closely with God. When men are put under such pressure they tend to curse and seek revenge. Stephen was different and we should follow his example.

Gazing at death may be a terrifying thing, but gazing past death to the presence of Jesus who is waiting to receive the righteous is the hope that dispels all fear. This is where Stephen was in this prayer. Jesus also looked beyond the cross to the glory of His Father and, like Stephen, requested God to receive His spirit, because He was in constant touch with His Father. Stephen was the same: he was able to see Jesus through his pain and suffering: *"I see heaven open and the Son of Man standing at the right hand of God"* (**Acts 7:56**). This is how God desires us to be. To see beyond our pain, troubles and challenges right into the heart of His son, Jesus Christ.

By getting close to God in our prayer life we have the opportunity to glorify God, even in the face of death. Stephen did not pray for his killers to be consumed by fire. Instead, he asked God to forgive them for their sin. This can only happen when we see Jesus in our affliction. Pray that God may open your eyes to His glory in the midst of your suffering. That way, your prayers will change. For Stephen, the glory of God was so strong that he wanted his spirit to connect with the Father. This is the prayer of a true believer, one who is not afraid or hesitant to leave this world for a life with Jesus.

Stephen teaches us that a true walk with God cannot be affected by the suffering of the body. If we stand for righteousness and truth, God will turn up in our time of need and give us an opportunity to be with Him.

REFLECT AND PRAY

What do you make of Stephen's passion and example? Please read his speeches and look at his life so you can begin to emulate him. Ask the Lord for a passion like Stephen's, and for his mercy and compassion so that you can forgive those that cause you pain and sorrow. Ask for the grace to even forgive those who may wish to kill you.

26

CORNELIUS' PRAYER

❦

"At Caesarea there was a man named Cornelius, a centurion in what was known as the Italian Regiment. He and all his family were devout and God-fearing; he gave generously to those in need and prayed to God regularly. One day at about three in the afternoon he had a vision. He distinctly saw an angel of God, who came to him and said, 'Cornelius!' Cornelius stared at him in fear. 'What is it, Lord?' he asked. The angel answered, 'Your prayers and gifts to the poor have come up as a memorial offering before God.'"
– Acts 10:1-4 –

An angel came to Cornelius and told him that his prayers had come up as a memorial before God. A memorial is a record. It is also defined as a statement of facts, especially as the basis of a petition. A memorial is also a structure that is established to remind others of a person or an event. In this case, Cornelius's prayers were so consistent in reminding God of certain issues that God sent an angel to encourage him and show him how to play a part in the answer to his own prayers. As a result, the Holy Spirit was given to the Gentiles in Cornelius's city – Caesarea.

We are not told what this man was praying for; all we know is that his prayers were so effective that an angel was dispatched to let him know that his prayers had made it to the throne of God. But judging by the results in Acts 10, we can surmise that

Cornelius was praying for the people of Caesarea. **Revelation 5:8** tells us that the prayers of God's people do make it to heaven: *"... the four living creatures and the twenty-four elders fell down before the Lamb. Each one had a harp and they were holding golden bowls full of incense, which are the prayers of God's people."* God's people are all those who truly believe in Him – whether Jew or Gentile. Be encouraged by the fact that your prayers are kept in heaven, provided you are a believer. Cornelius was a devout man who feared God. He was a believer. **Revelation 8:4** also tells us: *"The smoke of the incense, together with the prayers of God's people, went up before God from the angel's hand."*

The apostle Peter describes believers in this way: *"But you are a chosen people, a royal priesthood, a holy nation, God's special possession, that you may declare the praises of him who called you out of darkness into his wonderful light"* (**1 Peter 2:9**). This passage adds to the things we must focus on for our prayers to make it before God. It is the prayers of the believers, the holy ones, the devout worshippers, and those that fear God that are answered. Your character and conduct matters before God if you want to have fellowship with Him. Cornelius's life demonstrated the genuineness of his devotion to God: he gave generously to those in need, and the angel noted this.

Prayer is a means of fellowship between men and a holy God. Let us learn from Cornelius how to conduct our day-to-day living while we pray, so that our prayers may be answered like his were. An angel was eventually dispatched to encourage Cornelius and his family. May the Lord encourage you and send you hope as you continue to pray. Reading the whole account will show us how God answered this man's prayers, and hopefully help us learn from him.

Reflect and Pray

How is your lifestyle? Are you making an effort to fear God? Are you making an effort to live a holy life? That might just be a way for you to receive your answer. Begin to fear and honour God in your life.

27

PAUL PRAYS FOR HIMSELF

❦

*"Therefore, in order to keep me from becoming
conceited, I was given a thorn in my flesh, a messenger
of Satan, to torment me. Three times I pleaded with the
Lord to take it away from me. But he said to me, 'My
grace is sufficient for you, for my power is made perfect in
weakness.'"*

– 2 Corinthians 12:7-9 –

Many Bible commentators have tried to identify the thorn Paul was praying about, but none of them can arrive at a certain conclusion because Paul decided to keep it private. All we know about this problem is that it was very uncomfortable. It affected the apostle's ego and confidence. He claims that this was given to him deliberately, to keep him humble.

The other thing we pick up from this passage is the pain that this thorn brought. It tormented him! The apostle also considered it a messenger from Satan. This was a difficult situation and the apostle pleaded with the Lord three times for this satanic thorn to be taken away from him. This was the essence of his prayer: *"Lord, please remove this painful thing from me."* The three times of pleading Paul is talking about may not have happened all in one day. To me, it suggests that the effect of this thorn was so severe that it drove the apostle to pray for its removal on three separate occasions – probably three intensive sessions of prayer.

The Lord did not grant him his request, but chose to assure him that there was enough grace for him to endure this pain: *"My grace is sufficient for you, for my power is made perfect in weakness"* (verse 9). God will not always remove things that trouble us when we ask Him to do so. In this case, we learn that although our requests may not be granted, there will be sufficient grace for us to go through the pain and the torment without falling. I don't know what your thorn could be but when you pray, there will be sufficient grace for you to carry on. You will not fall, you will not fail and you will not lose your salvation, because the Lord will grant the necessary grace for you to pass through the difficult time.

Different people experience different thorns. For some, it could be failure to conceive and bear children. For others, it could be difficulty to find a marriage partner. For others, it could be a very uncomfortable and wearisome marriage. For others, it could be the failure to get a job. For some, it could be related to immigration status. There are many thorns trying to torment us, day in and day out. We should take them to the Lord in prayer. If we learn to do that, He will give us the grace we need to carry us through.

After prayer, the apostle had an understanding that the presence of this difficult challenge kept him humble, prayerful and close to God. Learn not to lose heart because of supposedly 'unanswered' prayer. God may just have chosen to grant you enough grace in that situation to spare your soul. *"For what shall it profit a man, if he shall gain the whole world, and lose his own soul?"* (**Mark 8:36**, KJV). Remember that God is more concerned about your soul than the material and physical benefits of this world. His grace is sufficient for you!

Reflect and Pray

Forgiveness comes from the Master. He forgives as He wills. Pray that you may learn to accept God's grace towards others. Pray for humility. Do not question God in His dealings with people. Ask God for the grace to be grateful for your own forgiveness, no matter how small, because you could still never pay for it.

28

PAUL PRAYS FOR THE PHILIPPIANS

❦

"And this is my prayer: that your love may abound more and more in knowledge and depth of insight, so that you may be able to discern what is best and may be pure and blameless for the day of Christ, filled with the fruit of righteousness that comes through Jesus Christ—to the glory and praise of God."
– Philippians 1:9-11 –

Paul was not praying for material blessings and provision for this church in these verses. He aimed for something greater, something eternal, and something that would ultimately please God. This is a prayer for godly character and transformation of the heart that can come only through Christ Jesus, as the prayer indicates.

God wants us to be like Him. This is the most important of all prayers for any believer or disciple, that we might fully attain the image of God. God is love and Paul wants our love to abound so we may be like God. He mentions knowledge and insight and the ability to discern what is best. This is not mediocre Christianity; these are deep character formations that develop godliness.

In verse 10 Paul prays that the Philippians might be *"pure"*, or as the King James Version puts it, *"sincere"*. Sincerity can be granted by God as He works with our hearts. It comes *"through Jesus Christ"* (verse 11). Many believers lack sincerity and purity these days. One reason is that many of us do not see it as important, so we do not even pray about it. But Paul was not like that; he understood that sincerity is part of the attributes that glorify God. Learn to pray for sincerity in your heart and those you minister to. Sincerity means pure, unmixed with other things and free from falsehood. Looking at the lives of many who claim to be believers is disappointing due to their insincerity and lack of purity. In some congregations people do not trust one another due to the lack of sincerity and integrity.

Paul also prayed in verse 11 that the believers may be *"blameless"* or *"without offence"* (KJV). This means not leading others to sin by one's own behaviour. A high expectation indeed! Our lives must not suggest anything evil for others. We must not be their reason to sin or fall.

When last did you pray like this for yourself? When last did you put the interests of others first (**Philippians 2:4**)? This can only happen when we are filled with the *"fruit of righteousness"*, as Paul prayed (verse 11). This should be our prayer guide when we pray for the church daily. Ask for the fruit of righteousness to fill us as believers. The prayers we have been studying should broaden our scope in prayer. There is more to prayer than asking for safe travel and personal needs. There is more to prayer than asking for success in studies and a good job. This is what Paul teaches us in his prayers.

Finally, Paul desires all these attributes not just for the Philippians, but also for every believer. He wants us to live like this till *"the day of Christ"* (verse 10). This means we should live our lives in such a manner till we die.

REFLECT AND PRAY

How far are you from these points that Paul is raising? Ask God to help you live up to this prayer in knowledge, discernment, sincerity, righteousness, abounding more and more in love. You can become what Paul prayed about if you begin to desire it and consciously focus on it day-by-day, prayer-by-prayer.

29

PAUL PRAYS FOR THE EPHESIANS

ᕕᕐᕗᕐᕕᕐᕕ

"For this reason I kneel before the Father, from whom every family in heaven and on earth derives its name. I pray that out of his glorious riches he may strengthen you with power through his Spirit in your inner being, so that Christ may dwell in your hearts through faith. And I pray that you, being rooted and established in love, may have power, together with all the Lord's holy people, to grasp how wide and long and high and deep is the love of Christ, and to know this love that surpasses knowledge—that you may be filled to the measure of all the fullness of God."

– Ephesians 3:14-19 –

Paul's mission and ministry as an apostle was to enlighten all people about the mystery of God's grace and love. He did this by preaching, teaching and praying for them. This mystery was not understood in previous times but it had become clearer with the coming of Jesus Christ. Paul did not understand at first either, as witnessed by his persecution of Christians (**Acts 8:1-3**).

In this prayer, he is sharing his experiences and knowledge (and the mystery) of Jesus Christ. He wants the Ephesians to have the same revelation and understanding: *"I pray that out of his glorious riches he may strengthen you with power through his Spirit in your inner being..."* (verse 16). How often do we pray such prayers? Do you realise that you have an inner being that needs to be strengthened? Paul also prays that Christ would dwell in their hearts through faith (verse 17). Does Christ dwell in your heart by faith? Maybe it is time you prayed such prayers and see what having Christ dwell in you by faith means.

Like he prayed for the Philippians, Paul also desires that this church would be rooted and grounded in love (verse 17). Love featured a lot in Paul's prayers, and understandably so, because Christ was the epitome of God's love. Paul's prayers for the Ephesians are connected with the heart and character of Jesus. This is important because that is how disciples are made – by imitating Jesus. *"Follow my example, as I follow the example of Christ"*, Paul said (**1 Corinthians 11:1**). How did Paul imitate Christ? He did so by his lifestyle and his prayers, as we can see in this passage.

Paul desired that Christ might dwell in our hearts through faith. This is what Jesus is looking for. Speaking to John in **Revelation 3:20**, Jesus said, *"I stand at the door and knock. If anyone hears my voice and opens the door, I will come in and eat with that person, and they with me."* This is the heart and the will of Jesus, to dwell in us through faith. Jesus demonstrated this in His speeches in the Gospel of John (**chapters 14–17**). This prayer teaches us how to pray for the churches and our Christian brothers and sisters. We must pray that we may fully comprehend the love of Jesus. The fact that this love surpasses knowledge is the reason why we need help in understanding it. How would you understand giving water to your enemies? This is not natural. It is beyond our common knowledge, and we can only comprehend it by the help of the Holy Spirit. This is what this prayer is about.

To be able to shine the light of faith in our communities, we must be filled with all the fullness of God, as Paul prayed. This fullness of God can make us sons of God that can speak the will of the Father. But we cannot just be filled with this presence of God while lying on our backs and sipping tea. We get it on our knees in prayer. That is the only way to get results from God. We must walk closely with God and continue to pray and feed from the Word. This is what Paul says in **Ephesians 4:1**: *"I urge you to live a life worthy of the calling you have received."* A believer's life should match the excellency of Christ's calling, and this can only happen when Christ dwells in our hearts.

REFLECT AND PRAY

Are you grounded in the love of God? Are you strong in your inner being? Do you fully comprehend the width, the breadth and the height of the love of Christ? Pray and ask God to give you understanding. He answers prayers.

30

HUSBANDS' PRAYER

*"Husbands, in the same way be considerate as you
live with your wives, and treat them with respect as the
weaker partner and as heirs with you of the gracious gift
of life, so that nothing will hinder your prayers."*
– 1 Peter 3:7 –

This passage shows us important ingredients for answered
prayer as husbands. Christian husbands are to demonstrate
the unselfish heart of Christ to their wives. The Christian
husband is called upon to be intimately aware of his wife's
needs, her strengths, her weaknesses, her goals and her desires.
He should know all these things so that he can respond to them
in the best possible way, whilst giving her honour in the process.
This is so important because failure to do this could cause a
husband's prayers to be hindered.

This is a very sobering scripture. Here the apostle Peter is
implying that every husband is supposed to be praying for his
wife. I hope if you are a husband you are praying for your wife,
because no one else can pray exactly the same way for her as
you can, as you should know her best. The important lesson in
this scripture is that a husband's prayers will not be answered
if he chooses to abuse his wife. The way a Christian husband is
answered by God when he prays is directly related to the way
he treats his wife.

Why did Peter raise this problem and link it with prayer?
Because God is interested in our godliness and He wants us to
treat our wives the same way He treats the Church. He also

wants us to be like Him in the way we treat our families. He believes this to be so important that our prayers can be hindered if we don't obey. Two lessons from the Apostle Peter are that God expects the husbands to pray. He also expects them to live with their wives with understanding. If they fail to do so, God is prepared to close His ears to their prayers.

Maybe you have been praying for years without answers, progress or change. Just look into your relationship with your wife and check if you follow what Peter is saying here. It might be the reason why you have not been answered. When your prayers have not been answered it affects your destiny and that of your family.

REFLECT AND PRAY

Ask your wife how you have conducted yourself. If you have not been treating her well, repent and ask the Lord to forgive you. Also ask for forgiveness from your wife. Start to treat her as God expects you to and live with your wife with understanding. If you are not a husband, pray for husbands and ask the Lord to help them to love their wives and live well with them. Should you consider becoming a husband in the future, determine and pray that you will treat your future wife well.

ABOUT THE AUTHOR

Osien Sibanda is an ordained minister of the Gospel. He is the senior pastor of God's House International Centre Bristol. He is an inspiring, gifted teacher of the Word of God. His experience in working with different denominations and people from various cultural backgrounds has broadened his capacity to work effectively with people. Pastor Osien is a conference speaker and a mentor of men. His passion is to see men taking responsibility in their homes, communities and churches. Pastor Osien was involved in church planting in Southern Africa and has done pastoral work in the UK. He also served as the Chairperson of Agape Husbands for four successive years in Johannesburg, South Africa.

He graduated with a Masters degree in Practical Theology from the University of Wales-Bangor. He is the author of *The Principles and Practice of Giving, The God Told Me Syndrome, Count the Cost, The Value Of Kindness,* and Devotional books which are: *The Pursuit Of God, The Parables of Jesus and The Miracles of Jesus.* Pastor Osien is married to Fatima and they are blessed with two lovely daughters, Ayanda and Realeboga.

OTHER BOOKS FROM SIBANDA PUBLISHING

BY FATIMA SIBANDA

The Fragrance of a Godly Woman
ISBN: 978-0-9561175-0-2

Daughter Arise! Defy Your Limitations and Scale the Utmost Height
ISBN: 978-0-9561175-4-0

Your Path is Becoming Brighter
ISBN: 978-0-9561175-7-1

You Can Do A Beautiful Thing!
ISBN: 978-0-9935446-1-3

BY OSIEN SIBANDA

The Principles and Practice of Giving
ISBN: 978-0-9561175-1-9

The God Told Me Syndrome
ISBN: 978-0-9561175-2-6

Count the Cost
ISBN: 978-0-9561175-3-3

The Value of Kindness
ISBN: 978-0-9561175-6-4

30 DAY DEVOTIONALS

The Parables of Jesus
ISBN: 978-0-9561175-9-5

The Pursuit of God
ISBN: 978-0-9561175-8-8

The Miracles of Jesus
ISBN: 978-0-9935446-0-6

All books are available to order online worldwide
through Amazon and other major book retailers!

For more information please contact
info@sibandapublishing.com

Lightning Source UK Ltd.
Milton Keynes UK
UKHW020240240120
357502UK00005B/365

9 780993 544620